The Thinking Tree

HOBBY FA
WRITING
STORY BUILDING
VOCABULARY & GRAMMAR

For Creative & Active Kids

CREATIVE LANGUAGE ARTS
WORD GAMES, PHONICS LESSONS, SENTENCE STRUCTURE,
PRONUNCIATION ACTIVITIES, CREATIVE WRITING & STORY PROMPTS

By: Sarah Janisse Brown

We use the Dyslexie Font by Christian Boer

The Thinking Tree Publishing Company, LLC

FunSchooling. com

Copyright 2025

Reproducible for Family Use Only

FUN-SCHOOLING
WITH THINKING TREE BOOKS

Story, Curriculum Design & Illustrations

by Sarah Janisse Brown

This book is set in the Dyslexie Font,

designed by Christian Boer

Copyright © 2025

Standard License

This book is licensed for: Personal and family use

Reproducible use with up to five students
in co-ops, micro-schools, or private tutoring.

For classroom use with more than five students,
a school license is required.

Published by:

The Thinking Tree , LLC

Phone: 317.622.8852

Name:

SILLY SENTENCES
SIMPLE STORIES
& PUNCHY POEMS

Before you start this book read some great poetry
about life on the homestead, nature, animals, hobbies, and more!
Ready? It's time to try writing your own!

YOUR CHALLENGE
IF YOU CHOOSE TO ACCEPT IT!

(or if your mom or teacher says you must!)

Your challenge is to come up with
creative and funny sentences, sweet little stories,
or poems inspired by life on the farm, animals and hobbies.

TO MAKE THINGS EVEN MORE FUN, YOULL GET:

- A picture to spark ideas.
- A list of words that sound alike to help your writing pop!

STORY BUILDING STARTS WITH
FINDING THE BEST WORDS

Before we start, here's a quick reminder of some important parts of speech—and a few goofy farm examples to make you smile:

NOUNS:

A noun is a person, place, thing, or idea.

Example: The <u>goat</u> sat on the <u>tractor</u> and <u>licked</u> a pineapple.

VERBS:

A verb is an action word—it tells what someone or something is doing.

Example: The pig <u>danced</u> in the mud while the chickens <u>sang</u>.

ADJECTIVES:

An adjective describes a noun.

It tells you more about it—like its color, size, shape, or personality.

Example: The <u>tiny</u>, <u>grumpy</u> rooster wore sparkly boots.

On the next few pages we have provided cheat sheets! Anytime you are in search of a great work, flip to the word section.

NOUNS

air	butter	dough	fields	harvest
arm	candle	dream	fire	head
autumn	can	drip	flavor	heap
baby	care	drop	flowers	herb
ball	chair	duckling	food	hill
barn	chicken	duck	forest	honey
bed	chores	dust	friends	hour
bee	clock	ears	garden	hue
bees	clucks	earth	gardens	hug
bell	coats	egg	geese	jam
belly	color	elderberry	gift	jars
birds	coop	everywhere	giggles	jelly
blackberry	cornflower	eyes	goose	job
block	cough	fabric	goat	joy
bloom	cousin	face	gold	kid
bounty	dad	fall	grace	kitchen
boy	dawn	family	grandma	kitten
branch	day	farm	grandpa	lamb
bread	days	father	grass	leaf
breakfast	dew	feed	gratitude	leaves
breath	dinner	feet	ground	Lettuce
breeze	dirt	fellow	group	lemon
brother	distance	fence	hall	light
brown	door	field	hand	limp

NOUNS

mama	pastures	seeds	strength	trust
map	patio	shade	stuff	truth
maple	pie	shape	summer	tummy
marshmallow	pill	shed	sun	vegetable
might	plate	shoes	sunshine	warmth
milk	pleasure	side	syrup	wax
mint	poo	sill	table	way
mom	puddles	sister	tables	weeks
moments	rain	skies	tale	wick
morning	ramps	sky	taste	wiggle
mornings	recipe	sneeze	tea	wind
mother	roof	soil	thing	window
mud	rooster	song	things	winds
mushrooms	root beer	sounds	tick	winter
name	sage	spring	time	willow
nature	salad	sprout	tock	wool
night	salt	stain	toes	world
nose	sap	stance	tongue	worms
oak	sauce	steak	trays	yarn
oven	scene	stems	treasure	year
pancake	scraps	strain	tree	years
pasture	season	strawberry	truck	yeast

  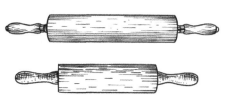 

PRESENT-TENSE VERBS

add	fall	need	sow
bake	fear	nibble	spend
bask	feed	note	sprinkle
be	feel	perch	sprout
believe	fill	mulch	stack
boil	flow	pick	stand
bolt	fly	plant	start
bounce	fold	plow	step
breathe	follow	pour	stir
bring	forage	pray	stitch
carry	gather	press	stop
chase	give	prune	streak
check	grow	put	swallow
churn	hang	raise	tap
clean	harvest	rake	taste
climb	heal	run	tell
collect	hear	scratch	think
come	help	seem	toss
cook	hum	share	trust
cough	jump	shine	turn
cover	keep	should	unfold
create	laugh	simmer	wait
crow	leave	sing	wake
dig	let	skip	walk
drink	make	sleep	wash
drip	mash	slide	watch
dry	mend	sneeze	water
eat	name	snuffle	weed

PAST-TENSE VERBS

added	feared	nibbled	spent
ate	fed	noted	sprinkled
baked	felt	opened	sprouted
basked	filled	perched	stacked
believed	flowed	picked	stood
boiled	flew	planted	started
bolted	folded	plowed	stepped
bounced	followed	poured	stirred
breathed	foraged	prayed	stitched
brought	gathered	pressed	stopped
came	gave	pruned	streaked
carried	grew	raised	swallowed
chased	harvested	raked	tasted
checked	healed	ran	tapped
churned	heard	said	took
cleaned	helped	sang	told
climbed	hummed	scratched	thought
collected	Hung	seemed	tossed
cooked	jumped	shared	trusted
coughed	kept	shone	turned
covered	laughed	should	unfolded
created	left	simmered	waited
crowed	let	skipped	woke
dug	made	slept	walked
drank	mashed	slid	washed
dripped	mended	sneezed	watched
dried	named	snuffled	watered
fell	needed	sowed	weeded

PRESENT PARTICIPLE VERBS

adding	fearing	nibbling	spending
baking	feeding	noting	sprinkling
basking	feeling	perching	sprouting
believing	filling	mulching	stacking
boiling	flowing	picking	standing
bolting	flying	planting	starting
bouncing	folding	plowing	stepping
breathing	following	pouring	stirring
bringing	foraging	praying	stitching
carrying	gathering	pressing	stopping
chasing	giving	pruning	streaking
checking	growing	putting	swallowing
churning	hanging	raising	taking
cleaning	harvesting	raking	taping
climbing	healing	running	tasting
collecting	hearing	saying	telling
coming	helping	scratching	thinking
cooking	humming	seeming	tossing
coughing	jumping	sharing	trusting
covering	keeping	shining	turning
creating	laughing	simmering	unfolding
crowing	leaving	singing	waiting
digging	letting	skipping	waking
drinking	making	sleeping	walking
dripping	mashing	sliding	washing
drying	mending	sneezing	watching
eating	naming	snuffling	watering
falling	needing	sowing	weeding

ADJECTIVES

aching	every	low	slippy
barefoot	fake	mellow	slow
better	fat	messy	small
biggest	finished	muddy	smitten
blooming	first	natural	soft
bright	fluffy	new	special
brittle	fresh	normal	speckled
broken	full	old	spicy
brown	glowing	pale	stormy
clean	golden	past	strong
cold	green	proud	sweet
cozy	high	second	tall
delicious	homemade	shiny	tart
done	little	shy	third
dotted	loud	slight	three

CREATE A FUNNY STORY, POEM, TOUNG-TWISTER, OR SILLY SENTENCE

Pick a Letter:_____

Choose a collection of Nouns, Verbs and Adjectives. Need ideas? Flip to the front of this book for help finding words that begin or end with this letter.

NOUNS	ADJECTIVES	VERBS
_____	_____	_____
_____	_____	_____
_____	_____	_____
_____	_____	_____
_____	_____	_____

Use some words that include this phonetic sound:

-op

toyshop	plop
crop	workshop
shop	raindrop
drop	eavesdrop
top	woodshop
stop	mop
hop	tiptop

TITLE:

_____

_____
_____
_____
_____
_____
_____
_____
_____
_____
_____
_____
_____
_____
_____
_____

CREATE A FUNNY STORY, POEM, TOUNG-TWISTER, OR SILLY SENTENCE

Pick a Letter:_____

Choose a collection of Nouns, Verbs and Adjectives. Need ideas? Flip to the front of this book for help finding words that begin or end with this letter.

NOUNS   ADJECTIVES   VERBS

_____   _____   _____

_____   _____   _____

_____   _____   _____

_____   _____   _____

_____   _____   _____

Use some words that include this phonetic sound:

-en

hen	happen
pen	tighten
glen	loosen
den	ripen
garden	brighten
open	listen

TITLE:

_____

_____

_____

_____

_____

_____

_____

_____

_____

_____

_____

_____

_____

_____

_____

_____

CREATE A FUNNY STORY, POEM, TOUNG-TWISTER, OR SILLY SENTENCE

Pick a Letter:_____

Choose a collection of Nouns, Verbs and Adjectives. Need ideas? Flip to the front of this book for help finding words that begin or end with this letter.

NOUNS	ADJECTIVES	VERBS
_____	_____	_____
_____	_____	_____
_____	_____	_____
_____	_____	_____
_____	_____	_____

Use some words that include this phonetic sound:

-ick

chick	trick
pick	sidekick
brick	candlestick
stick	prick
wick	quick
flick	homesick
kick	click

TITLE:

_____

_____
_____
_____
_____
_____
_____
_____
_____
_____
_____
_____
_____
_____
_____
_____

CREATE A FUNNY STORY, POEM, TOUNG-TWISTER, OR SILLY SENTENCE

Pick a Letter:_____

Choose a collection of Nouns, Verbs and Adjectives. Need ideas? Flip to the front of this book for help finding words that begin or end with this letter.

NOUNS	ADJECTIVES	VERBS
_____	_____	_____
_____	_____	_____
_____	_____	_____
_____	_____	_____
_____	_____	_____

Use some words that include this phonetic sound:

-ill

hill	will
grill	until
spill	instill
chill	overkill
thrill	windmill
fill	landfill
bill	refill

TITLE:

_____

_____

_____

_____

_____

_____

_____

_____

_____

_____

_____

_____

_____

_____

_____

_____

_____

_____

CREATE A FUNNY STORY, POEM, TOUNG-TWISTER, OR SILLY SENTENCE

Pick a Letter:_____

Choose a collection of Nouns, Verbs and Adjectives. Need ideas? Flip to the front of this book for help finding words that begin or end with this letter.

NOUNS	ADJECTIVES	VERBS
_____	_____	_____
_____	_____	_____
_____	_____	_____
_____	_____	_____
_____	_____	_____

Use some words that include this phonetic sound:

-ash

cash	stash
flash	ash
splash	whiplash
slash	rehash
crash	newsflash

TITLE:

_____

_____
_____
_____
_____
_____
_____
_____
_____
_____
_____
_____
_____
_____
_____
_____
_____
_____
_____
_____
_____
_____

CREATE A FUNNY STORY, POEM, TOUNG-TWISTER, OR SILLY SENTENCE

Pick a Letter:_____

Choose a collection of Nouns, Verbs and Adjectives. Need ideas? Flip to the front of this book for help finding words that begin or end with this letter.

NOUNS	ADJECTIVES	VERBS
_____	_____	_____
_____	_____	_____
_____	_____	_____
_____	_____	_____
_____	_____	_____

Use some words that include this phonetic sound:

-all

stall	nightfall
ball	**install**
call	snowfall
small	downfall
fall	recall
wall	windfall

TITLE:

_____

CREATE A FUNNY STORY, POEM, TOUNG-TWISTER, OR SILLY SENTENCE

Pick a Letter:_____

Choose a collection of Nouns, Verbs and Adjectives. Need ideas? Flip to the front of this book for help finding words that begin or end with this letter.

NOUNS   ADJECTIVES   VERBS

_____   _____   _____

_____   _____   _____

_____   _____   _____

_____   _____   _____

_____   _____   _____

Use some words that include this phonetic sound:

-ark

bark	bookmark
park	remark
mark	stark
spark	watermark
dark	disembark
embark	hallmark

TITLE:

_____

_____

_____

_____

_____

_____

_____

_____

_____

_____

_____

_____

_____

_____

_____

_____

_____

_____

_____

CREATE A FUNNY STORY, POEM, TOUNG-TWISTER, OR SILLY SENTENCE

Pick a Letter:_____

Choose a collection of Nouns, Verbs and Adjectives. Need ideas? Flip to the front of this book for help finding words that begin or end with this letter.

NOUNS	ADJECTIVES	VERBS
_____	_____	_____
_____	_____	_____
_____	_____	_____
_____	_____	_____
_____	_____	_____

Use some words that include this phonetic sound:

-ell

bell

smell

farewell

sell

dwell

spell

tell

yell

TITLE:

_____

_____
_____
_____
_____
_____
_____
_____
_____
_____
_____
_____
_____

CREATE A FUNNY STORY, POEM, TOUNG-TWISTER, OR SILLY SENTENCE

Pick a Letter:_____

Choose a collection of Nouns, Verbs and Adjectives. Need ideas? Flip to the front of this book for help finding words that begin or end with this letter.

NOUNS	ADJECTIVES	VERBS
_____	_____	_____
_____	_____	_____
_____	_____	_____
_____	_____	_____
_____	_____	_____

Use some words that include this phonetic sound:

-ent

tent

vent

scent

bent

event

talent

different

silent

TITLE:

_____

_____

_____

_____

_____

_____

_____

_____

_____

_____

_____

_____

_____

_____

_____

_____

CREATE A FUNNY STORY, POEM, TOUNG-TWISTER, OR SILLY SENTENCE

Pick a Letter:_____

Choose a collection of Nouns, Verbs and Adjectives. Need ideas? Flip to the front of this book for help finding words that begin or end with this letter.

NOUNS	ADJECTIVES	VERBS
_____	_____	_____
_____	_____	_____
_____	_____	_____
_____	_____	_____
_____	_____	_____

Use some words that include this phonetic sound:

-er

butter

sweeter

ladder

farmer

hamster

rancher

faster

better

TITLE:

_____

_____

_____

_____

_____

_____

_____

_____

_____

_____

_____

_____

_____

_____

_____

_____

_____

CREATE A FUNNY STORY, POEM, TOUNG-TWISTER, OR SILLY SENTENCE

Pick a Letter:_____

Choose a collection of Nouns, Verbs and Adjectives. Need ideas? Flip to the front of this book for help finding words that begin or end with this letter.

NOUNS   ADJECTIVES   VERBS

_____   _____   _____

_____   _____   _____

_____   _____   _____

_____   _____   _____

_____   _____   _____

Use some words that include this phonetic sound:

-ate

crate

plate

create

celebrate

decorate

late

date

TITLE:

_____

_____

_____

_____

_____

_____

_____

_____

_____

_____

_____

_____

_____

_____

_____

_____

_____

CREATE A FUNNY STORY, POEM, TOUNG-TWISTER, OR SILLY SENTENCE

Pick a Letter:_____

Choose a collection of Nouns, Verbs and Adjectives. Need ideas? Flip to the front of this book for help finding words that begin or end with this letter.

NOUNS	ADJECTIVES	VERBS
_____	_____	_____
_____	_____	_____
_____	_____	_____
_____	_____	_____
_____	_____	_____

Use some words that include this phonetic sound:

-eat

treat

wheat

heat

seat

beat

eat

defeat

heartbeat

preheat

TITLE:

_____

_____
_____
_____
_____
_____
_____
_____
_____
_____
_____
_____
_____
_____
_____
_____
_____
_____

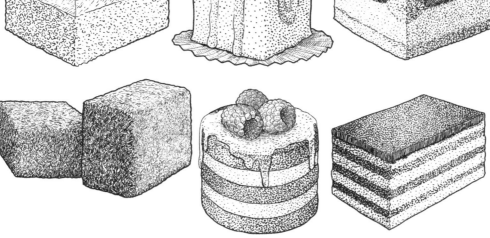

CREATE A FUNNY STORY, POEM, TOUNG-TWISTER, OR SILLY SENTENCE

Pick a Letter:_____

Choose a collection of Nouns, Verbs and Adjectives. Need ideas? Flip to the front of this book for help finding words that begin or end with this letter.

NOUNS	ADJECTIVES	VERBS
_____	_____	_____
_____	_____	_____
_____	_____	_____
_____	_____	_____
_____	_____	_____

Use some words that include this phonetic sound:

-eet

meet

greet

beet

feet

sweet

sheet

tweet

street

bittersweet

TITLE:

_____

_____
_____
_____
_____
_____
_____
_____
_____
_____
_____
_____
_____
_____
_____
_____
_____
_____
_____

CREATE A FUNNY STORY, POEM, TOUNG-TWISTER, OR SILLY SENTENCE

Pick a Letter:_____

Choose a collection of Nouns, Verbs and Adjectives. Need ideas? Flip to the front of this book for help finding words that begin or end with this letter.

NOUNS	ADJECTIVES	VERBS
_____	_____	_____
_____	_____	_____
_____	_____	_____
_____	_____	_____
_____	_____	_____

Use some words that include this phonetic sound:

-ine

vine

pine

line

twine

line

shine

decline

combine

define

TITLE:

_____

_____
_____
_____
_____
_____
_____
_____
_____
_____
_____
_____
_____
_____
_____

CREATE A FUNNY STORY, POEM, TOUNG-TWISTER, OR SILLY SENTENCE

Pick a Letter:_____

Choose a collection of Nouns, Verbs and Adjectives. Need ideas? Flip to the front of this book for help finding words that begin or end with this letter.

NOUNS	ADJECTIVES	VERBS
_____	_____	_____
_____	_____	_____
_____	_____	_____
_____	_____	_____
_____	_____	_____

Use some words that include this phonetic sound:

-ock

sock

block

flock

clock

dock

rock

unlock

restock

gridlock

TITLE:

_____

_____
_____
_____
_____
_____
_____
_____
_____
_____
_____
_____
_____
_____
_____
_____
_____
_____

CREATE A FUNNY STORY, POEM, TOUNG-TWISTER, OR SILLY SENTENCE

Pick a Letter:_____

Choose a collection of Nouns, Verbs and Adjectives. Need ideas? Flip to the front of this book for help finding words that begin or end with this letter.

NOUNS	ADJECTIVES	VERBS
_____	_____	_____
_____	_____	_____
_____	_____	_____
_____	_____	_____
_____	_____	_____

Use some words that include this phonetic sound:

-ore

core

explore

store

shore

more

adore

galore

ignore

TITLE:

_____

_____

_____

_____

_____

_____

_____

_____

_____

_____

_____

_____

_____

_____

_____

_____

_____

_____

CREATE A FUNNY STORY, POEM, TOUNG-TWISTER, OR SILLY SENTENCE

Pick a Letter:_____

Choose a collection of Nouns, Verbs and Adjectives. Need ideas? Flip to the front of this book for help finding words that begin or end with this letter.

NOUNS	ADJECTIVES	VERBS
_____	_____	_____
_____	_____	_____
_____	_____	_____
_____	_____	_____
_____	_____	_____

Use some words that include this phonetic sound:

-ose

rose

hose

nose

close

those

suppose

propose

compose

enclose

TITLE:

CREATE A FUNNY STORY, POEM, TOUNG-TWISTER, OR SILLY SENTENCE

Pick a Letter:_____

Choose a collection of Nouns, Verbs and Adjectives. Need ideas? Flip to the front of this book for help finding words that begin or end with this letter.

NOUNS	ADJECTIVES	VERBS
_____	_____	_____
_____	_____	_____
_____	_____	_____
_____	_____	_____
_____	_____	_____

Use some words that include this phonetic sound:

-own

town

crown

gown

brown

frown

down

breakdown

meltdown

shutdown

TITLE:

_____

CREATE A FUNNY STORY, POEM, TOUNG-TWISTER, OR SILLY SENTENCE

Pick a Letter:_____

Choose a collection of Nouns, Verbs and Adjectives. Need ideas? Flip to the front of this book for help finding words that begin or end with this letter.

NOUNS	ADJECTIVES	VERBS
_____	_____	_____
_____	_____	_____
_____	_____	_____
_____	_____	_____
_____	_____	_____

Use some words that include this phonetic sound:

-out

sprout

scout

trout

about

layout

shout

lookout

wipeout

TITLE:

_____

_____
_____
_____
_____
_____
_____
_____
_____
_____
_____
_____
_____
_____
_____
_____
_____
_____

CREATE A FUNNY STORY, POEM, TOUNG-TWISTER, OR SILLY SENTENCE

Pick a Letter:_____

Choose a collection of Nouns, Verbs and Adjectives. Need ideas? Flip to the front of this book for help finding words that begin or end with this letter.

NOUNS	ADJECTIVES	VERBS
_____	_____	_____
_____	_____	_____
_____	_____	_____
_____	_____	_____
_____	_____	_____

Use some words that include this phonetic sound:

-our

flour

devour

hour

our

scour

sour

TITLE:

_____

_____

_____

_____

_____

_____

_____

_____

_____

_____

_____

_____

CREATE A FUNNY STORY, POEM, TOUNG-TWISTER, OR SILLY SENTENCE

Pick a Letter:_____

Choose a collection of Nouns, Verbs and Adjectives. Need ideas? Flip to the front of this book for help finding words that begin or end with this letter.

NOUNS	ADJECTIVES	VERBS
_____	_____	_____
_____	_____	_____
_____	_____	_____
_____	_____	_____
_____	_____	_____

Use some words that include this phonetic sound:

-OW

meadow

window

blow

glow

yellow

shadow

know

TITLE:

CREATE A FUNNY STORY, POEM, TOUNG-TWISTER, OR SILLY SENTENCE

Pick a Letter:_____

Choose a collection of Nouns, Verbs and Adjectives. Need ideas? Flip to the front of this book for help finding words that begin or end with this letter.

NOUNS	ADJECTIVES	VERBS
_____	_____	_____
_____	_____	_____
_____	_____	_____
_____	_____	_____
_____	_____	_____

Use some words that include this phonetic sound:

-OW

cow

clow

allow

chow

meow

now

how

somehow

TITLE:

_____

_____

_____

_____

_____

_____

_____

_____

_____

_____

_____

_____

_____

_____

_____

_____

_____

_____

_____

CREATE A FUNNY STORY, POEM, TOUNG-TWISTER, OR SILLY SENTENCE

Pick a Letter:_____

Choose a collection of Nouns, Verbs and Adjectives. Need ideas? Flip to the front of this book for help finding words that begin or end with this letter.

NOUNS	ADJECTIVES	VERBS
_____	_____	_____
_____	_____	_____
_____	_____	_____
_____	_____	_____
_____	_____	_____

Use some words that include this phonetic sound:

-ink

drink

clink

pink

blink

stink

link

sink

TITLE:

_____

CREATE A FUNNY STORY, POEM, TOUNG-TWISTER, OR SILLY SENTENCE

Pick a Letter:_____

Choose a collection of Nouns, Verbs and Adjectives. Need ideas? Flip to the front of this book for help finding words that begin or end with this letter.

NOUNS	ADJECTIVES	VERBS
_____	_____	_____
_____	_____	_____
_____	_____	_____
_____	_____	_____
_____	_____	_____

Use some words that include this phonetic sound:

-ing

planting

hiking

grilling

gardening

camping

fishing

TITLE:

_____

_____

_____

_____

_____

_____

_____

_____

_____

_____

_____

_____

CREATE A FUNNY STORY, POEM, TOUNG-TWISTER, OR SILLY SENTENCE

Pick a Letter:_____

Choose a collection of Nouns, Verbs and Adjectives. Need ideas? Flip to the front of this book for help finding words that begin or end with this letter.

NOUNS	ADJECTIVES	VERBS
_____	_____	_____
_____	_____	_____
_____	_____	_____
_____	_____	_____
_____	_____	_____

Use some words that include this phonetic sound:

-oud

cloud

loud

proud

aloud

shroud

TITLE:

_____

_____
_____
_____
_____
_____
_____
_____
_____
_____
_____
_____
_____
_____

CREATE A FUNNY STORY, POEM, TOUNG-TWISTER, OR SILLY SENTENCE

Pick a Letter:_____

Choose a collection of Nouns, Verbs and Adjectives. Need ideas? Flip to the front of this book for help finding words that begin or end with this letter.

NOUNS	ADJECTIVES	VERBS
_____	_____	_____
_____	_____	_____
_____	_____	_____
_____	_____	_____
_____	_____	_____

Use some words that include this phonetic sound:

-ound

ground

sound

mound

round

pound

hound

found

TITLE:

_____

_____
_____
_____
_____
_____
_____
_____
_____
_____
_____
_____
_____
_____

CREATE A FUNNY STORY, POEM, TOUNG-TWISTER, OR SILLY SENTENCE

Pick a Letter:_____

Choose a collection of Nouns, Verbs and Adjectives. Need ideas? Flip to the front of this book for help finding words that begin or end with this letter.

NOUNS	ADJECTIVES	VERBS
_____	_____	_____
_____	_____	_____
_____	_____	_____
_____	_____	_____
_____	_____	_____

Use some words that include this phonetic sound:

-ight

night

might

height

plight

delight

right

flight

light

TITLE:

_____

_____

_____

_____

_____

_____

_____

_____

_____

_____

_____

_____

CREATE A FUNNY STORY, POEM, TOUNG-TWISTER, OR SILLY SENTENCE

Pick a Letter:_____

Choose a collection of Nouns, Verbs and Adjectives. Need ideas? Flip to the front of this book for help finding words that begin or end with this letter.

NOUNS	ADJECTIVES	VERBS
_____	_____	_____
_____	_____	_____
_____	_____	_____
_____	_____	_____
_____	_____	_____

Use some words that include this phonetic sound:

-ike

bike

like

trike

hike

spike

alike

dislike

TITLE:

_____

_____

_____

_____

_____

_____

_____

_____

_____

_____

_____

_____

CREATE A FUNNY STORY, POEM, TOUNG-TWISTER, OR SILLY SENTENCE

Pick a Letter:_____

Choose a collection of Nouns, Verbs and Adjectives. Need ideas? Flip to the front of this book for help finding words that begin or end with this letter.

NOUNS	ADJECTIVES	VERBS
_____	_____	_____
_____	_____	_____
_____	_____	_____
_____	_____	_____
_____	_____	_____

Use some words that include this phonetic sound:

-et

basket

hatchet

blanket

market

pocket

gadget

pet

TITLE:

_____

_____
_____
_____
_____
_____
_____
_____
_____
_____
_____
_____

CREATE A FUNNY STORY, POEM, TOUNG-TWISTER, OR SILLY SENTENCE

Pick a Letter:_____

Choose a collection of Nouns, Verbs and Adjectives. Need ideas? Flip to the front of this book for help finding words that begin or end with this letter.

NOUNS	ADJECTIVES	VERBS
_____	_____	_____
_____	_____	_____
_____	_____	_____
_____	_____	_____
_____	_____	_____

Use some words that include this phonetic sound:

-ook

cookbook

nook

look

book

cook

look

outlook

notebook

TITLE:

_____

_____
_____
_____
_____
_____
_____
_____
_____
_____
_____
_____

CREATE A FUNNY STORY, POEM, TOUNG-TWISTER, OR SILLY SENTENCE

Pick a Letter:_____

Choose a collection of Nouns, Verbs and Adjectives. Need ideas? Flip to the front of this book for help finding words that begin or end with this letter.

NOUNS	ADJECTIVES	VERBS
_____	_____	_____
_____	_____	_____
_____	_____	_____
_____	_____	_____
_____	_____	_____

Use some words that include this phonetic sound:

-ny

bunny

tiny

enemy

sunny

penny

funny

many

TITLE:

_____

_____
_____
_____
_____
_____
_____
_____
_____
_____
_____
_____
_____
_____
_____
_____
_____

CREATE A FUNNY STORY,
POEM, TOUNG-TWISTER,
OR SILLY SENTENCE

Pick a Letter:_____

Choose a collection of Nouns, Verbs and Adjectives. Need ideas? Flip to the front of this book for help finding words that begin or end with this letter.

NOUNS	ADJECTIVES	VERBS
_____	_____	_____
_____	_____	_____
_____	_____	_____
_____	_____	_____
_____	_____	_____

Use some words that include this phonetic sound:

-oy

toy

enjoy

boy

destroy

annoy

joy

employ

TITLE:

_____

_____

_____

_____

_____

_____

_____

_____

_____

_____

_____

CREATE A FUNNY STORY, POEM, TOUNG-TWISTER, OR SILLY SENTENCE

Pick a Letter:_____

Choose a collection of Nouns, Verbs and Adjectives. Need ideas? Flip to the front of this book for help finding words that begin or end with this letter.

NOUNS	ADJECTIVES	VERBS
_____	_____	_____
_____	_____	_____
_____	_____	_____
_____	_____	_____
_____	_____	_____

Use some big words that include these tricky phonetic sounds:

-o	-ue	-ew
two	shoe	new
who	blue	view
to	glue	threw
too	true	chew
do	rescue	grew
undo	value	brew

TITLE:

_____

_____
_____
_____
_____
_____
_____
_____
_____
_____
_____
_____
_____
_____
_____

CREATE A FUNNY STORY, POEM, TOUNG-TWISTER, OR SILLY SENTENCE

Pick a Letter:_____

Choose a collection of Nouns, Verbs and Adjectives. Need ideas? Flip to the front of this book for help finding words that begin or end with this letter.

NOUNS	ADJECTIVES	VERBS
_____	_____	_____
_____	_____	_____
_____	_____	_____
_____	_____	_____
_____	_____	_____

Use some big words that include these tricky phonetic sounds:

-o	-ue	-ew
two	shoe	new
who	blue	view
to	glue	threw
too	true	chew
do	rescue	grew
undo	value	brew

TITLE:

_____

_____
_____
_____
_____
_____
_____
_____
_____
_____
_____
_____
_____
_____
_____
_____

CREATE A FUNNY STORY, POEM, TOUNG-TWISTER, OR SILLY SENTENCE

Pick a Letter:_____

Choose a collection of Nouns, Verbs and Adjectives. Need ideas? Flip to the front of this book for help finding words that begin or end with this letter.

NOUNS	ADJECTIVES	VERBS
_____	_____	_____
_____	_____	_____
_____	_____	_____
_____	_____	_____
_____	_____	_____

Use some big words that include these tricky phonetic sounds:

-ike

kite
invite
bite
brite
quite
invite

-ight

flight
light
night
sight
bright
right

TITLE:

_____

_____

_____

_____

_____

_____

_____

_____

_____

_____

_____

_____

_____

CREATE A FUNNY STORY, POEM, TOUNG-TWISTER, OR SILLY SENTENCE

Pick a Letter:_____

Choose a collection of Nouns, Verbs and Adjectives. Need ideas? Flip to the front of this book for help finding words that begin or end with this letter.

NOUNS	ADJECTIVES	VERBS
_____	_____	_____
_____	_____	_____
_____	_____	_____
_____	_____	_____
_____	_____	_____

Use some big words that include these tricky phonetic sounds:

-y

my
buy
try
cry
sky

-ie

pie
tie
die
lie
vie

TITLE:

_____

_____
_____
_____
_____
_____
_____
_____
_____
_____
_____
_____
_____
_____
_____

CREATE A FUNNY STORY, POEM, TOUNG-TWISTER, OR SILLY SENTENCE

Pick a Letter:_____

Choose a collection of Nouns, Verbs and Adjectives. Need ideas? Flip to the front of this book for help finding words that begin or end with this letter.

NOUNS	ADJECTIVES	VERBS
_____	_____	_____
_____	_____	_____
_____	_____	_____
_____	_____	_____
_____	_____	_____

Use some big words that include these tricky phonetic sounds:

-ine

clothesline
define
vine
mine
shine
dine

-ign

sign
design
align
assign
realign
malign

TITLE:

_____

_____
_____
_____
_____
_____
_____
_____
_____
_____
_____
_____
_____
_____
_____

CREATE A FUNNY STORY, POEM, TOUNG-TWISTER, OR SILLY SENTENCE

Pick a Letter:_____

Choose a collection of Nouns, Verbs and Adjectives. Need ideas? Flip to the front of this book for help finding words that begin or end with this letter.

NOUNS	ADJECTIVES	VERBS
_____	_____	_____
_____	_____	_____
_____	_____	_____
_____	_____	_____
_____	_____	_____

Use some big words that include these tricky phonetic sounds:

-ed

fed
shed
bed
red
led

-ead

bread
thread
dread
dead
read

TITLE:

_____

_____
_____
_____
_____
_____
_____
_____
_____
_____
_____
_____
_____
_____
_____

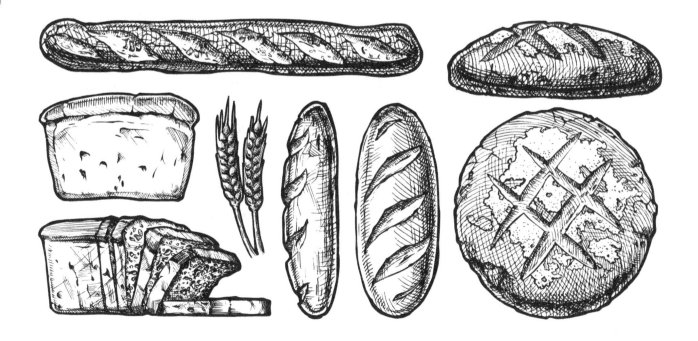

CREATE A FUNNY STORY, POEM, TOUNG-TWISTER, OR SILLY SENTENCE

Pick a Letter:_____

Choose a collection of Nouns, Verbs and Adjectives. Need ideas? Flip to the front of this book for help finding words that begin or end with this letter.

NOUNS	ADJECTIVES	VERBS
_____	_____	_____
_____	_____	_____
_____	_____	_____
_____	_____	_____
_____	_____	_____

Use some big words that include these tricky phonetic sounds:

-e	-ee	ea	-y	-ey
she	tree	tea	puppy	donkey
he	free	sea	happy	turkey
we	three	flea	silly	honey
me	see	pea	messy	money
me	bee		bunny	valley

TITLE:

_____

_____
_____
_____
_____
_____
_____
_____
_____
_____
_____
_____
_____
_____
_____
_____
_____

CREATE A FUNNY STORY, POEM, TOUNG-TWISTER, OR SILLY SENTENCE

Pick a Letter:_____

Choose a collection of Nouns, Verbs and Adjectives. Need ideas? Flip to the front of this book for help finding words that begin or end with this letter.

NOUNS	ADJECTIVES	VERBS
_____	_____	_____
_____	_____	_____
_____	_____	_____
_____	_____	_____
_____	_____	_____

Use some big words that include these tricky phonetic sounds:

-ees	-eze	-ase	-eas
bees	breeze	please	peas
trees	freeze	tease	seas
knees	sneeze	release	fleas

TITLE:

_____

_____

_____

_____

_____

_____

_____

_____

_____

_____

_____

_____

CREATE A FUNNY STORY, POEM, TOUNG-TWISTER, OR SILLY SENTENCE

Pick a Letter:_____

Choose a collection of Nouns, Verbs and Adjectives. Need ideas? Flip to the front of this book for help finding words that begin or end with this letter.

NOUNS	ADJECTIVES	VERBS
_____	_____	_____
_____	_____	_____
_____	_____	_____
_____	_____	_____
_____	_____	_____

Use some big words that include these tricky phonetic sounds:

-ire

campfire
desire
require

-ious

glorious
mysterious
victorious

-tion

emotion
commotion
devotion

-der

under
wonder
thunder

TITLE:

_____

_____
_____
_____
_____
_____
_____
_____
_____
_____
_____
_____
_____
_____
_____
_____
_____
_____

CREATE A FUNNY STORY, POEM, TOUNG-TWISTER, OR SILLY SENTENCE

Pick a Letter:_____

Choose a collection of Nouns, Verbs and Adjectives. Need ideas? Flip to the front of this book for help finding words that begin or end with this letter.

NOUNS	ADJECTIVES	VERBS
_____	_____	_____
_____	_____	_____
_____	_____	_____
_____	_____	_____
_____	_____	_____

Use some big words that include these tricky phonetic sounds:

-ire	-ious	-tion	-der
campfire	glorious	emotion	under
desire	mysterious	commotion	wonder
require	victorious	devotion	thunder

TITLE:

_____

_____

_____

_____

_____

_____

_____

_____

_____

_____

_____

_____

_____

_____

_____

_____

CREATE A FUNNY STORY,
POEM, TOUNG-TWISTER,
OR SILLY SENTENCE

Pick a Letter:_____

Choose a collection of Nouns, Verbs and Adjectives. Need ideas? Flip to the
front of this book for help finding words that begin or end with this letter.

NOUNS	ADJECTIVES	VERBS
_____	_____	_____
_____	_____	_____
_____	_____	_____
_____	_____	_____
_____	_____	_____

Use some big words that include these tricky phonetic sounds:

-ation

observation	revelation	vibration
creation	invitation	imagination
foundation	transformation	innovation
sensation	declaration	aspiration

TITLE:

_____

_____
_____
_____
_____
_____
_____
_____
_____
_____
_____
_____
_____
_____
_____

STORY BUILDING
FROM SCRATCH

START FROM SCRATCH

Write a poem or story about this picture:

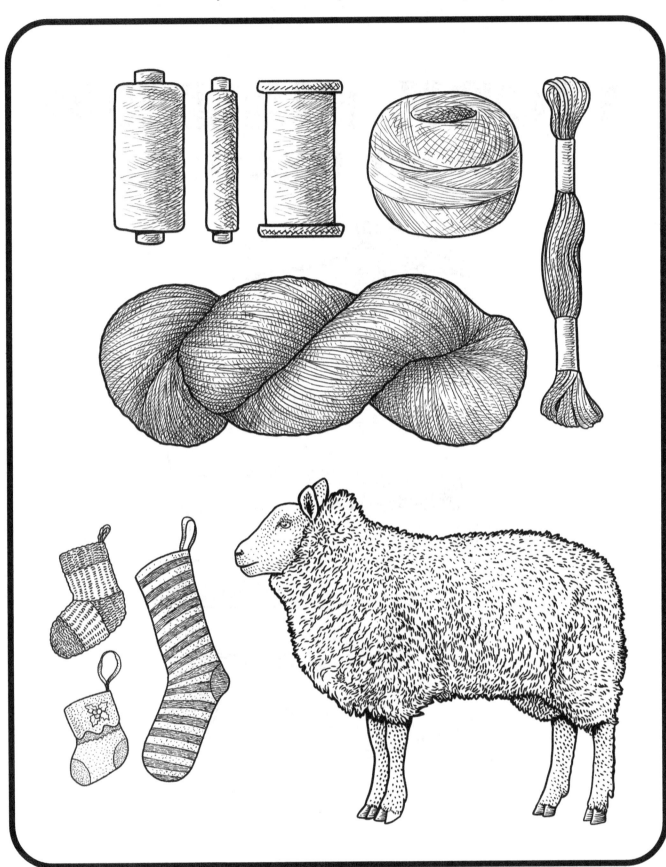

TITLE:

START FROM SCRATCH

Write a poem or story about this picture:

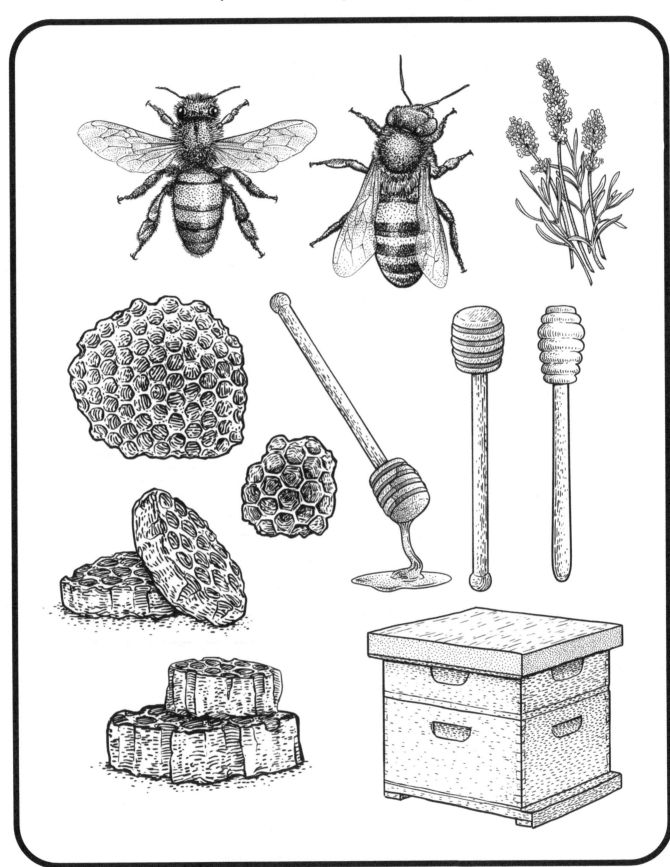

TITLE:

START FROM SCRATCH

Write a poem or story about this picture:

TITLE:

_____

START FROM SCRATCH

Write a poem or story about this picture:

TITLE:

START FROM SCRATCH

Write a poem or story about this picture:

TITLE:

START FROM SCRATCH

Write a poem or story about this picture:

TITLE:

_____

START FROM SCRATCH

Write a poem or story about this picture:

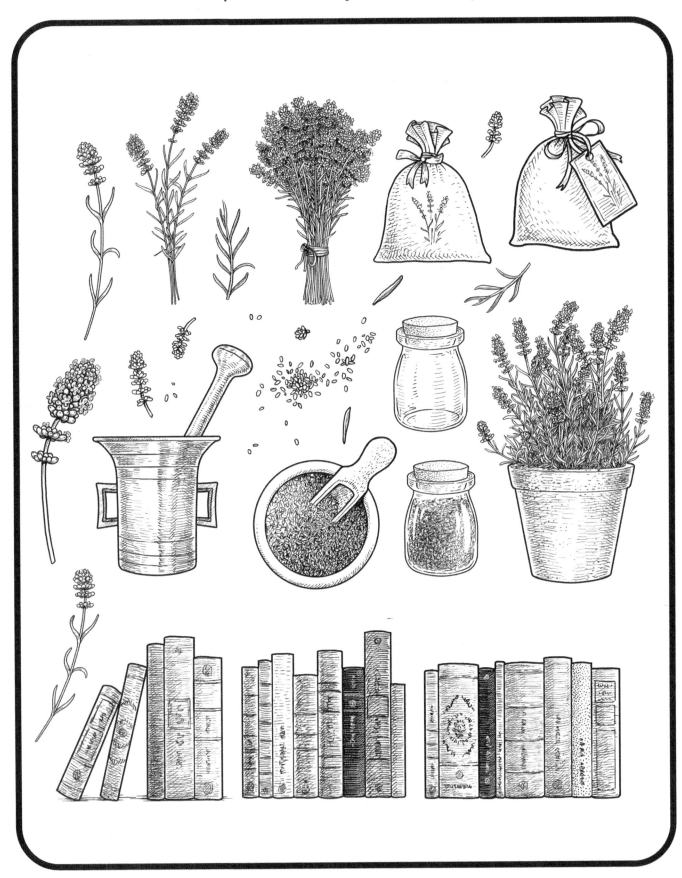

TITLE:

START FROM SCRATCH

Write a poem or story about this picture:

TITLE:

DO IT YOURSELF

Write a poem or story and add your own illustration:

TITLE:

DO IT YOURSELF

Write a poem or story and add your own illustration:

TITLE:

_____

DO IT YOURSELF

Write a poem or story and add your own illustration:

TITLE:

DO IT YOURSELF

Write a poem or story and add your own illustration:

TITLE:

DO IT YOURSELF

Write a poem or story and add your own illustration:

TITLE:

Made in the USA
Monee, IL
26 July 2025

21928810R00070